The Simple SCIENCE ACTIVITY BOOK

Jane Bull

Previously published as *Crafty Science*

Contents

Jane Bull

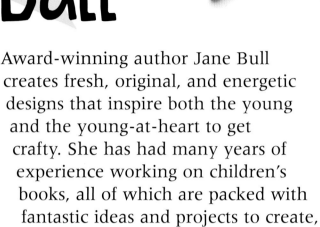

Award-winning author Jane Bull creates fresh, original, and energetic designs that inspire both the young and the young-at-heart to get crafty. She has had many years of experience working on children's books, all of which are packed with fantastic ideas and projects to create, including *Made by Me*, *Stitch-by-Stitch*, *Crafty Creatures*, and *Crafty Dolls*.

! Safety

ADULTS: You will need to supervise children **AT ALL TIMES** when performing the activities, especially near water. You will need to carry out the steps that require sharp knives, other potentially dangerous equipment, or a heat source. Additionally, an adult will need to apply any strong glue.

BEFORE YOU START:

- ❶ When you see this warning symbol, take extra care and ask an adult for help.

- Be careful around hot ovens, making sure you know whether the oven is on or not. Protect your hands when touching or lifting anything hot from, or on, or into an oven or stovetop. Oven mitts are your friends here!

- Always check that the ingredients for a recipe do not contain anything that you or a friend or anyone eating the dish might be allergic to or that are not otherwise part of your recommended diet.

Jules Pottle

Jules is an award-winning primary-school science teacher and author. She is passionate about making science learning hands-on, accessible, and exciting. Jules trains teachers in using stories to teach science and often presents at teaching conferences. She also writes picture books that teach science through story.

- Be careful handling sharp items, such as knives, scissors, pins, or skewers. Take extra care when using any of these.

- Take extra care when handling hot liquids or hot pans, being careful to avoid spills and protecting your hands (with oven mitts or a dish towel) when moving or holding them.

- Ask an adult for help with using strong glue, staplers, paper fasteners, and chemical liquids, such as vinegar and turpentine. Don't put anything into your mouth and wash your hands thoroughly after using any of these items.

- Never put small magnets in your mouth and put them safely away when you have finished the experiment.

- When using power tools, such as electric mixers, check if they're on, and don't put your hands near the moving parts until you have switched them off at the socket.

Casting shadows

shadows

You will need:

- A camera—a disposable one or a phone camera
- Some willing models
- Your imagination
- Lots of bright sunshine

View the world from some strange angles using shadows made by the sun, and then capture them on camera. If you are in a room with more than one light, you will have more than one shadow.

What's the science?

Shadows occur when an object **blocks the path of light rays**. The amount of light that is blocked depends on whether the object is **solid** or **transparent** (see-through). Solid objects cast the strongest shadows because most of the light rays are reflected back from the object's surface, creating a dark shadow. Transparent items, such as a glass bottle, let almost all the light through. They still cast a blurry shadow, mainly around the edges of the object.

Call me Turkey!

Special effects

Hand shadows against a wall are great, but why not use your whole body to create some really strange shadow effects? You can even base a story around your shadow photos.

Shadow clock

When an object blocks the light from the sun, a shadow is formed. You can use the shadow to tell the time! Make this clock to use outside on a sunny day.

When the sun is in the east, the shadows fall to the west.

What's the science?

Have you ever noticed how shadows grow longer or shorter depending on the time of day? **The shadow on your shadow clock is affected by how high the sun is in the sky.** The shadow starts off long, when the sun first comes over the horizon at dawn, gets shorter until noon, when the sun is overhead, and then grows long again as it drops below the horizon at sunset. Watch this happen on your shadow clock.

You will need:
- Paper plate
- Garden stake or stick
- Terra-cotta plant pot
- Mounting putty
- A watch
- Strips of paper

How to make a clock

Before you assemble your shadow clock, decorate the plate, stake, and pot.

1 Make a hole in the center of the plate and push the stake through.

Put some putty around the hole.

2 Now, put the stake through the hole in the plant pot.

Press the plate onto the putty.

3 Make sure the plate is a tight fit around the stake.

Use the sunlight to set your clock

You will need a whole sunny day to set your clock so that you can read it the next day.

1 Place your clock in a sunny area.

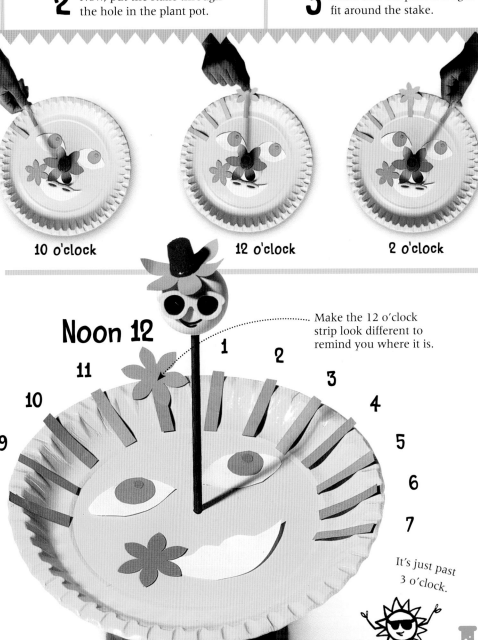

10 o'clock   12 o'clock   2 o'clock

2 The stake will cast a shadow across the plate. This is the sun telling you the time.

3 Now, look at your watch and mark the shadow on each hour with a strip of paper. For example, at 10 o'clock, mark the shadow, then continue until the sun goes down.

4 The next day, tell the time by seeing where the shadow falls!

Noon 12

Make the 12 o'clock strip look different to remind you where it is.

11   1   2
10   3
9   4
8   5
           6
           7

It's just past 3 o'clock.

While sharks have a very oily liver to help them stay afloat, bony fish have a swim bladder full of air to prevent them from sinking to the bottom of the sea.

Grrrrrrr

Let's move it!

Go, go, go!

What's the science?

So, what's floating your boat? The answer is **buoyancy**. Any object placed in water has two forces acting on it: its weight pulling it down and upthrust from the water pushing it up. If the object's weight is too much for the water to support, the object will **sink**. If it's lighter than the water, the object will **float**. The two bottles on your boat are full of air, which is very light. Fill them with sand or rice and see whether or not they still float.

Weight

Buoyancy

Keep your cool

What floats and what doesn't? It's a matter of life and death if there are vicious sharks in the water. Quick, get this boat out of here!

10

Make it float

Think, or you'll sink! All you need to remember is this: if it floats, it'll make a boat. Your boat will have to float if there are sharks around!

You will need:

Use anything you can find that floats for boat-building materials.

To make a basic boat

All you need is a plastic food container, two plastic bottles, scissors, and string. When you have finished, add special features, such as a control deck or a speedy spoiler.

! Ask an adult to help with the scissors.

Ask an adult to carefully make a hole in each corner, using scissors or a knife.

Plastic bottle

Plastic food container

Plastic bottle

Safety scissors and string

Thread string through each hole and tie tightly around each bottle.

! Ask an adult to supervise near water at all times.

11

Blowing bubbles

Bubbles are out of this world.

These shimmering spheres wobble into existence, float gently into the air, then disappear without a trace. That really is like magic!

To make really big bubbles, you will need:

- 4 cups water
- 5 tbsp concentrated dishwashing liquid
- 2 tbsp glycerin
- A large bowl • Wire
- Anything with holes in it!

Bubble recipe

Mix the dishwashing liquid, glycerin, and water in a bowl.

Blowing bubbles

Make your own bubble mixture, then search your house for things that you think you could blow bubbles through. Ask an adult to help you bend wire or old coat hangers into shapes to make your own blowers. You can make lots and lots of tiny bubbles or fewer huge ones.

What makes a good bubble?

A sphere has a smaller surface area than a cube that contains the same amount of air. The molecules in the bubble's filmy surface pull together as much as they can around the air inside, forming a sphere.

See what happens with a slotted spoon or strainer.

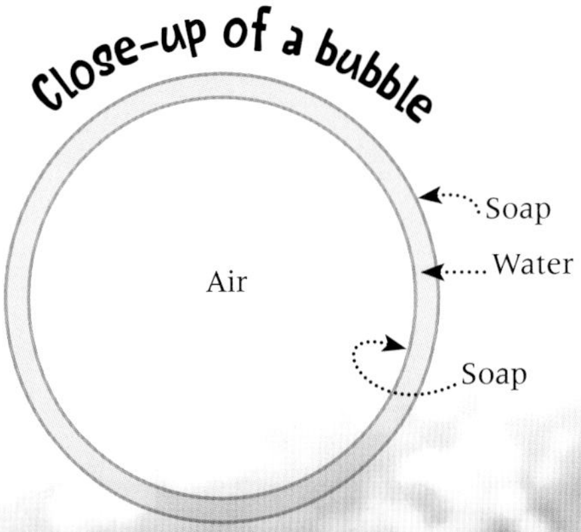

Close-up of a bubble

Soap

Water

Soap

Air

What is a bubble?

A bubble is just like a sandwich. Its skin has an inner and outer layer of soap with a thin layer of water in the middle.

See if you can blow bubbles with your hands.

Rainbow of colors!

Putting some cheesecloth over a tube makes a cloud of froth.

What's the science?

Bubbles only last as long as it takes the water to dry out, and then they pop. If you poke them, the water escapes much faster. If you blow bubbles on a hot day, they won't last long. On a cold day, they will hang around longer and float much higher because your warm breath is lighter than cold air. In icy weather, the bubbles may even freeze!

Chain reaction

You'll need a lot of force to knock all of these dominoes over... unless you start a chain reaction!

You will need:

- Safety scissors
- Cardboard tubes
- Tape
- Dominoes
- Toys

! **Ask an adult** to help with the scissors.

Start from a high point, such as a stool or box.

Push the first car down the ramp to start the chain reaction.

Tunnels and ramps can be made from cardboard tubes, either cut in half or whole.

It's a complete mess!

You can make the dominoes climb steps that aren't too high.

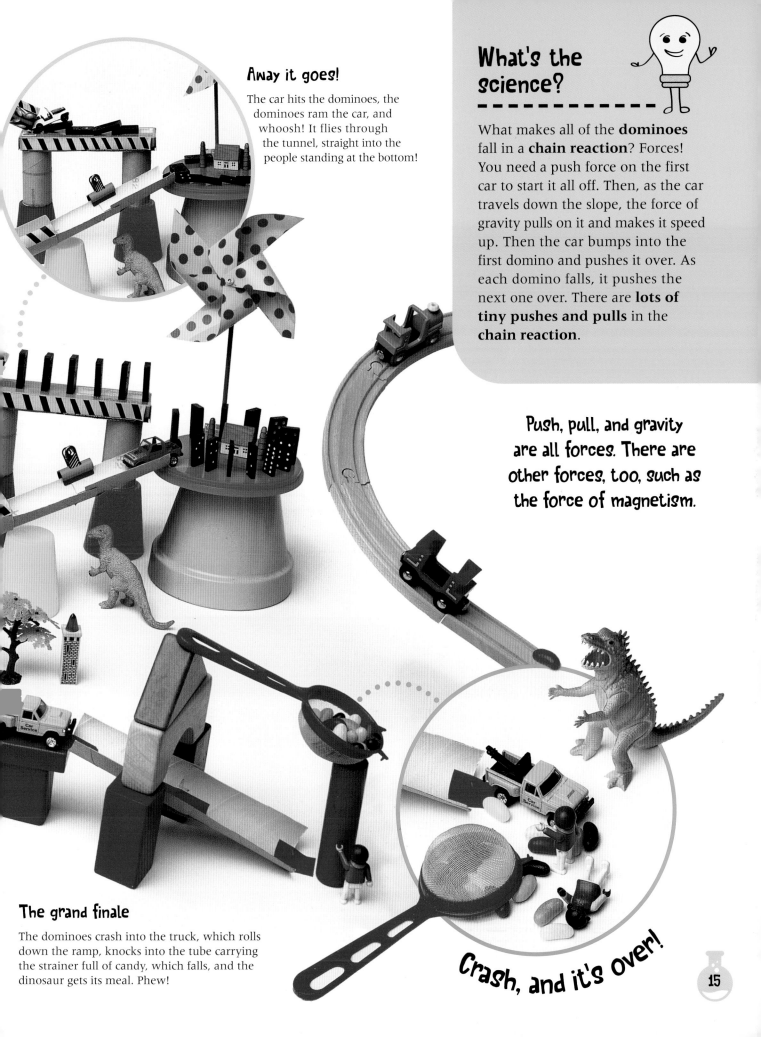

Away it goes!

The car hits the dominoes, the dominoes ram the car, and whoosh! It flies through the tunnel, straight into the people standing at the bottom!

What's the science?

What makes all of the **dominoes** fall in a **chain reaction**? Forces! You need a push force on the first car to start it all off. Then, as the car travels down the slope, the force of gravity pulls on it and makes it speed up. Then the car bumps into the first domino and pushes it over. As each domino falls, it pushes the next one over. There are **lots of tiny pushes and pulls** in the **chain reaction**.

Push, pull, and gravity are all forces. There are other forces, too, such as the force of magnetism.

The grand finale

The dominoes crash into the truck, which rolls down the ramp, knocks into the tube carrying the strainer full of candy, which falls, and the dinosaur gets its meal. Phew!

Crash, and it's over!

Falling snow

Shake up a storm

using just a screw-top jar, water, glycerin, glitter, and a few toys. Hold the jar still and watch the glittery snow fall down—the force of gravity is at work here!

! Ask an adult
to do the steps that require glue.

Take a jar

Choose a small jar with a very tight, screw-top lid. You may want to test it first—you don't want your snowstorms to leak everywhere.

1 Add glitter to the glycerin.

2 Fill the jar to the top with water.

3 Stir well.

Forces can make things move. Gravity pulls the glitter down.

! Glue tip

Ask an adult to use a strong glue that seals even when in water to fix the toy in place. For an extra seal, before they screw the lid shut, they can add some glue inside the rim of the lid to prevent leaks. Any excess glue must be wiped off carefully.

❶ Ask an adult to put glue around the inside of the lid and the outside of the jar rim.

Decorate the lid with festive ribbon.

What's the science?

Watch how the glitter in your snowstorm falls to the bottom of the jar. This happens because of **a force called gravity**, which **acts on everything in the universe**.

On Earth, gravity pulls everything toward the center of the planet. This is extremely useful because it stops things from flying off into space. No matter how many times you shake your snowstorm, **the glitter feels the pull of gravity** and settles when the water stops moving.

Glycerin

Glycerin is a nontoxic liquid that can be bought in most supermarkets and craft stores. It slightly thickens the water so that your glitter-snow falls more slowly when you shake it. Use about one cup of glycerin and two cups of water.

!4 Glue a toy onto the lid and leave to dry.

!5 Screw the lid on tightly.

6 Shake it up!

Frozen solid!

You can make a lantern out of water if you change the water from liquid water to solid ice by freezing it. Decorate your lantern with leaves and winter flowers. Place it outside to welcome guests, where your ice lantern will stay solid if the air is cold enough.

The big freeze

Position a small bowl inside a larger one and tape it so that the small bowl is hanging in the center—not touching the bottom or sides of the big bowl. Fill the large bowl with foliage and water, then freeze it.

Defrost tip

To remove the bowls, dip the frozen lantern in warm water and pour a little water into the smaller bowl as well, to loosen the ice.

If the small bowl bobs up too much, add some pebbles to weigh it down.

You will need:

- Large and small bowls
- Natural materials, such as leaves and flowers (ask an adult which are safe to use)
- Water
- Tape
- Candles
- Lids or containers
- String

Frosty glow

Use half a plastic bottle and a cup for the long lanterns, making sure that the cup doesn't touch the edges of the bottle. Use small or tall candles for the inside. If your frozen creation starts to defrost, perk it up by putting it back in the freezer.

You will need:

- Plastic bottle
- Plastic cup
- Tape
- Natural materials, such as leaves and flowers
- Candles
- Water

❗ Ask an adult to light the candles.

1 Fix the containers with tape so the cup is in the center of the bottle.

2 Arrange the plants in the gap between the cup and the bottle.

Ice art

Find some lids or containers with at least a ½-in (1-cm) tall rim and fill them with water. Put plant material into the lid, then drape the ends of a long piece of string into the water—they will freeze inside the ice. Put the lid into the freezer until it is frozen. Hang the decorations outside on trees or bushes.

Tape the string to the sides of the lid to keep it in place while the water freezes.

What's the science?

Ice is the solid form of water. When the temperature goes down to 32°F (0°C), water starts to freeze and become hard. It forms a hard crystal called ice. You may find that your fingers stick to your lantern as you try to get it out of the bowls. This is because the **moisture that is naturally on your hands starts to freeze onto the ice**, gluing your fingers against it. A little warm water will unstick them.

If you are turning out your lantern in a warm room, **the ice may be slippery**. This is because some of the water molecules on the surface of the ice are turning back into a liquid. This thin layer of water makes the ice hard to grip. **As more of the ice melts, the surface gets slipperier.**

3 Fill the gap with water, taking care not to disturb the plant material.

4 Freeze the bottle for several hours. Remove the bottle and the cup.

❗5 Place a tea light or candle inside the ice and ask an adult to light it.

Growing grasses!

Plants are amazing. They make their own food, using water, air, and the energy from sunlight. So, all you need to do to grow some long grassy hair on these heads is to supply those three things. The plant will do the rest.

! **Ask an adult**
to help with the scissors.

1. Cut out a 12 in (30 cm) strip from old pantyhose.

2. Tie a knot in one end. Turn the hose inside out.

3. Place a handful of grass seed inside.

4. Fill the rest of the sack with sawdust and tie a knot in the top.

5. Pinch out a nose and tie it with a rubber band.

6. Soak the head in a bowl of water until it is completely wet.

Keep your hair on!

Once you have prepared your head, place it upright in a dish. Make sure the nose is in the right place—remember, grass always grows upward. Sprinkle it with water daily, and when the hair has gone wild, give it a haircut.

The grass seeds are now at the top.

You will need:

- Safety scissors
- Pantyhose
- Grass seeds
- Sawdust
- Rubber band
- Gravel
- Plant pot
- Soil
- A bowl of water
- A dish

Create a face. Stick on eyes and other features.

Plants combine carbon dioxide (from the air) and water to make cellulose, using sunlight energy. This process is called photosynthesis.

Grow these any time!

Plant your pot

Place some gravel in the bottom of the pot, fill the pot with soil, and sprinkle a handful of seeds on top. Keep the pot damp and in a warm, light place, and, whatever you do, don't let the hair get out of control!

What's the science?

There are thousands of different types of grass, many of which we use as **food**—wheat, rice, and corn are all edible grasses. Animals eat grasses, too. Luckily, the **growing point** of the grass is at the base of the blade, so animals can grab a mouthful without damaging the plant, which quickly regrows. So, however many times you cut your plant's hair, it will grow back again!

Roots and shoots

Roots go down and shoots go up.
Let's see if beans know which way to grow.

Try these any time of year.

Which beans will you plant?

Butter   Kidney   Cannellini   Black-eyed pea   Navy   Soy   Aduki

❶ Bean machines

Place a selection of dried beans in a glass, fill the glass with water, and soak the beans well overnight. Don't eat them—dried beans are poisonous! Prepare another glass with damp paper towels wrapped around the inside. When your beans have finished soaking, carefully place them around the edge.

You will need:

- Dried beans
- 2 glasses
- Paper towels
- Water

Make sure you cover the beans in water when you soak them.

Who won the race? Which bean was fastest?

The bean husk is still hanging on.

The race is on!

After about two days, the beans will begin to sprout. Do the roots grow down and shoots go up? What happens if you turn the bean upside down? Remember to keep the beans moist.

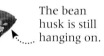

Keep the paper moist.

Mixed beans

Mung beans

Mustard seeds

Cress seeds

If you let a seed sprout and then upend it in the pot, the shoot will bend around to grow toward the light and the root will grow toward the ground.

A good crop

Try your hand at growing wheat grains. These grains came from a local farm. The seed grows into wheat and then produces grain, which is used to make bread. You could grow whole wheat, rye, or barley. Soak the grains overnight in a glass and then simply lay them on damp paper towels. Keep the paper towels moist and watch your wheat field grow.

What's the science?

Seeds need water to **begin to grow**. When you soak the seeds, they will swell up as they absorb water. The seed husk will also **soften and break open**. Then the root and shoot can get out. This is called **germination**. Plants always know which way is up. How do they do this? **Roots and shoots** each have a job to do, so they figure out which way to grow to get what they need. **Plants need water and nutrients from soil.** The tiny roots respond to the pull of gravity by growing down toward the center of the Earth, digging themselves into the soil. **Shoots need light and air to make food.** They sense the warmth of the sun above them, so they grow toward the light.

Soak the grains overnight before laying them on damp paper towels.

Check that the paper is moist every day.

Sweet tomatoes

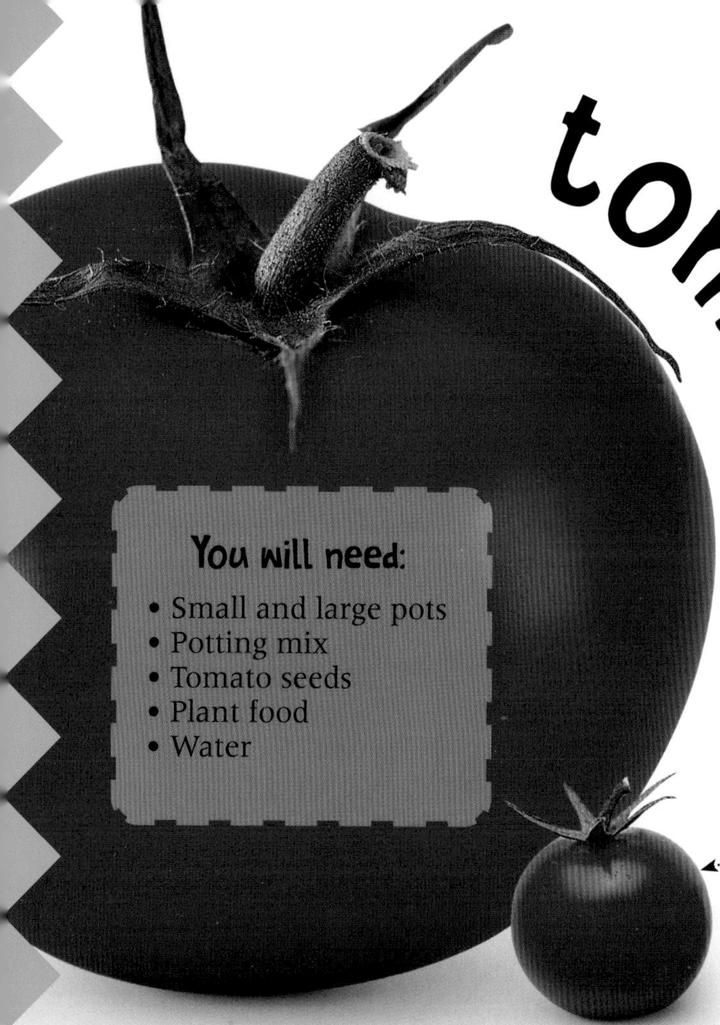

Tiny tomatoes. Big taste! Look for small varieties, such as cherry tomatoes. They not only taste the sweetest, but the plants also grow to just 16 in (40 cm) high. This will allow you to grow them in small pots and you won't need stakes to support them.

You will need:

- Small and large pots
- Potting mix
- Tomato seeds
- Plant food
- Water

The tiny, sweet tomatoes are the best for tasty, bite-sized snacks.

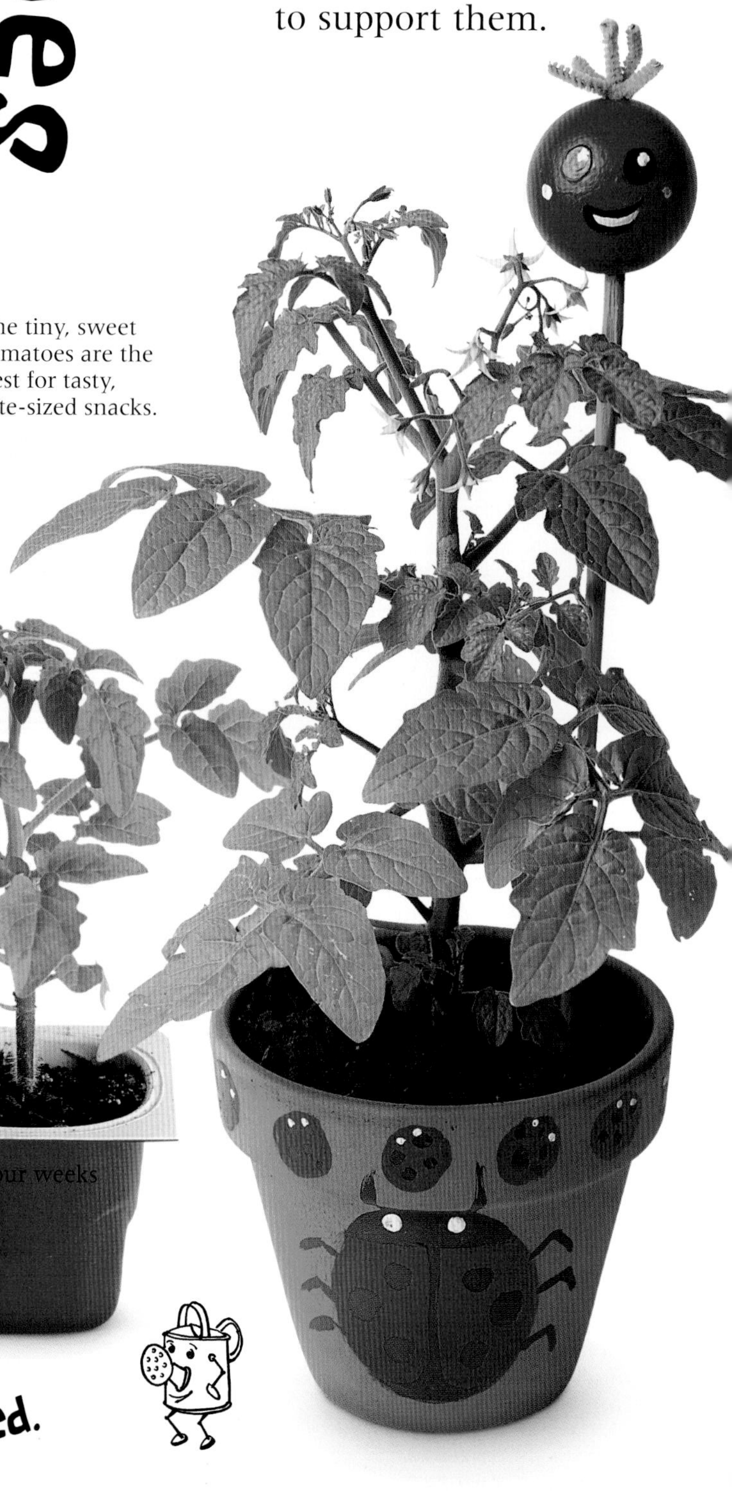

Growing a plant

1 Fill a small pot with potting mix. Push a seed into the center, just below the soil.

2 Place the pot on a windowsill and give it some water. Check it every day to make sure the soil is moist. In about a week, the plant should start to sprout.

3 When the plant has outgrown the pot, carefully move it to a bigger one.

4 Feed it with plant food, water it regularly, and wait for flowers to appear.

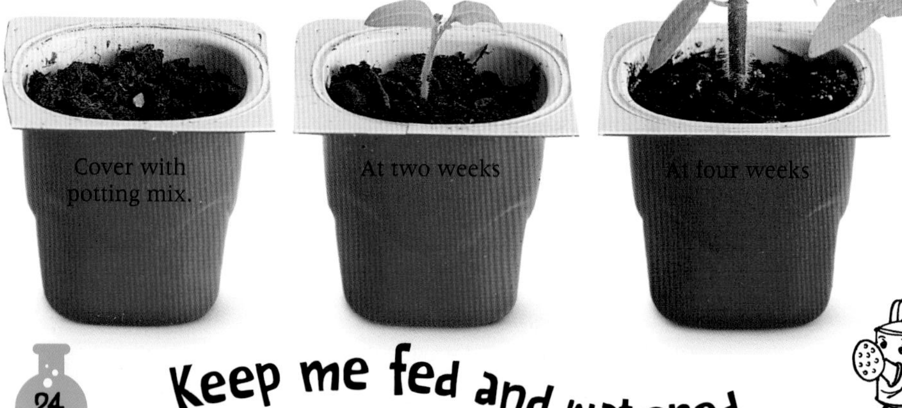

Cover with potting mix.
At two weeks
At four weeks

Keep me fed and watered.

When you see flowers

you'll know the fruit is on its way. The flowers disappear and the baby tomatoes grow in their place. After a few weeks, the fruit will ripen.

Start sowing

seeds in early spring.

Tomatoes are the fruit of the tomato plant because they contain the seeds.

Tomato tips

Planting seeds

Slice a tomato and scoop out the seeds. Dry them with paper towels, then plant them instead of using seeds from a packet. What do you think will happen?

Packet of tomato seeds

Ladybug friends

If you see a ladybug on your tomato plant, don't move it. Ladybugs are your friends. They eat the greenfly that want a bite of your tomato plants.

Tomato snacks

Wait until the tomatoes are completely red, then pick them, wash them, and eat them as snacks. You will find that your homegrown tomatoes are the tastiest of all.

What's the science?

If you brush the **hairs on a tomato stem**, you will notice that they are slightly sticky. There is a reason for this—**the stems are used to trap insects**. An insect gets stuck and dies, then wind, rain, or gravity pushes the insect onto the ground under the plant. Its body slowly breaks down, providing nutrients for the plant roots. Quite a lot of insects can be caught in this way. Potato plants, which are relatives of the tomato, do it, too.

senses garden

Scratch and sniff your way around some deliciously smelly plants.

Self-contained herb garden

Conjure an instant herb-garden-in-a-pot. Choose herbs for their smell, color, or taste. Decorate the container with a design that suits your little garden. Keep your herbs watered and in a warm, sheltered spot.

1 Pick four or five small plants.

2 Place small stones in the pot for drainage.

3 Add the plants and fill the pot with soil.

Chives ....

Decorate a Plant Pot.

Touchy-feely

The more you touch herbs, the more they give off their smell. Rub the leaves between your fingers and smell them.

Good scents

Every herb plant has its own special smell. Some are sweet, and some are sharp. Can you name the herb just by its smell?

Touch

Soft and furry

Crisp and curly

Sound

Stop! Listen

If your plants are outside, stop and listen for a moment. Can you hear buzzing? Bees love the fragrant flowers of herbs, such as thyme, lemon balm, and rosemary.

Taste

❗ Good taste

Herbs can help to make food taste even better. Ask and adult to chop up the leaves or use them whole.

Look out

Decorate your garden with painted pots and plant labels to show what's growing where.

Sight

These labels are made from table-tennis balls on sticks.

Water your plants regularly.

What's the science?

Herbs and many other plants, such as onions and garlic, have a particular smell. There are two reasons for this. **Some plants need to attract insects** to their flowers so that they can produce seeds to make new plants. In others, the **smell** and **taste** are there to **stop animals from eating them**. This keeps the plant from being damaged, so it can survive and grow bigger.

Catnip sock

Dried catnip

Create a face on a colorful sock using buttons and beads and fill the sock with catnip. Add rice or dried peas to make the sock heavier. Tie a knot and let your cat loose!

Smell

Marjoram

Cats have incredible senses of hearing and smell. They have whiskers that help them to feel their environment. The special reflective layer at the back of their eyes helps cats see in low light.

Parsley

Lemon balm

Apple mint

Sage

Reuse paper

Under, over, under, over. Don't throw paper away—turn it into art.
Weave pictures and turn them into cards or display them on the wall.

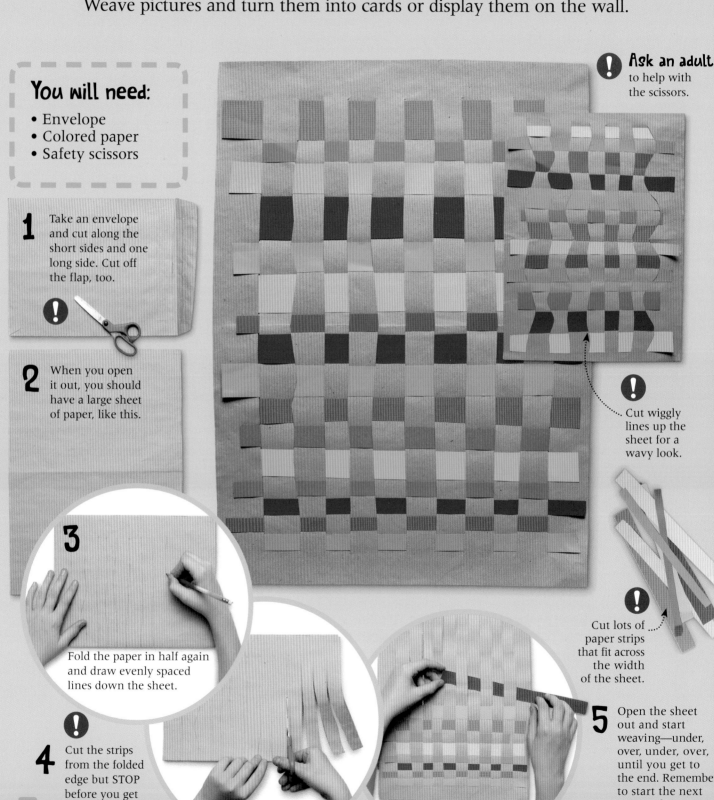

You will need:

- Envelope
- Colored paper
- Safety scissors

! **Ask an adult** to help with the scissors.

1 Take an envelope and cut along the short sides and one long side. Cut off the flap, too. **!**

2 When you open it out, you should have a large sheet of paper, like this.

! Cut wiggly lines up the sheet for a wavy look.

3 Fold the paper in half again and draw evenly spaced lines down the sheet.

! **4** Cut the strips from the folded edge but STOP before you get to the top.

! Cut lots of paper strips that fit across the width of the sheet.

5 Open the sheet out and start weaving—under, over, under, over, until you get to the end. Remember to start the next strip in the opposite way—over, under, over, under.

28

Under, over, under, over, weave, weave, weave

Picture weave

Use a picture from a magazine as your backing sheet, then weave plain strips along it.

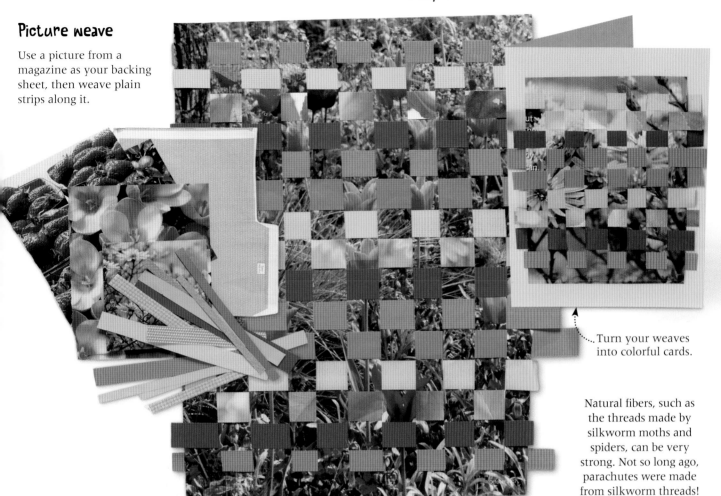

Turn your weaves into colorful cards.

Natural fibers, such as the threads made by silkworm moths and spiders, can be very strong. Not so long ago, parachutes were made from silkworm threads!

Experiment with patterned strips on a plain background.

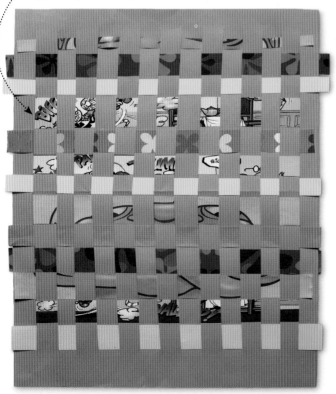

What's the science?

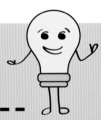

A thin strip of paper is reasonably **strong along its length**, but it is too narrow to hold or balance anything on it. However, if you interlace strips under and over **at right angles** to each other, they create a piece of paper that is strong, yet still **flexible**. This is because the strength in the length of the strip is now going across as well as up and down. A fabric loom uses the same idea by weaving strands of fabric together to create cloth. Very fine threads woven together can make a thin, but strong material.

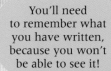

Invisible ink

Want to keep something secret?
Here's a way to stop your plans from falling into enemy hands. You don't need fancy spy equipment—all you need is a lemon!

You will need:

- Lemon • Bowl
- Paintbrush or cotton swabs • Paper
- An Iron

The acid in lemon juice is called citric acid. You also find it in sour candies and other citrus fruits.

Making ink

1 Squeeze a lemon into a bowl.

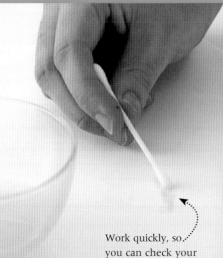

Work quickly, so you can check your text before it dries.

2 Write your secret message on the paper in lemon juice using a paintbrush or a cotton swab.

! **3** To decipher the message, ask an adult to iron the paper with a hot iron until the message comes through.

Book of secrets

Keep your secrets safe and sound in your very own secret-agent book. Take two pieces of cardboard and some paper, punch two holes down one side of them, and tie them together with a ribbon.

Tear the edges of the paper for an aged effect.

These secret messages will remain invisible to everyone.

Stick your secret messages into the book.

Rub a damp tea bag over your paper to make it look old.

! **Ask an adult** to help you with the iron— it gets hot!

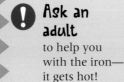

What's the science?

This trick works because **lemon juice is an acid**. When you put it on the paper, the **acid destroys some of the paper's surface**, so that when you heat the paper, the areas with the message turn brown first. If you don't have lemon juice, try this project using milk, which is also slightly acidic.

Stick on a strip of tape about 1 in (2 cm) long.

Don't inflate the balloon too much.

You will need:

- Long skewer or a pin • Clear tape
- Safety scissors • Balloon

Baffling balloons

Everyone knows that balloons pop if you stick something sharp into them. Show off your magical talents by skewering a balloon without it going BANG!

❗ Non-pop balloon

All you need for this amazing trick is some tape. Simply stick a piece on the balloon and, miraculously, you can poke a sharp stick or pin carefully through the tape. Prepare your balloon with tape before you perform your trick. Make sure to dispose of any broken pieces of the burst balloon. They can be harmful. Ask an adult to help with the skewer or pin.

What's the science?

Why doesn't the balloon **pop** when you skewer it? Balloons are made of stretchy **rubber**. As you **blow** into a balloon, the rubber **molecules** are **forced apart**, especially around the widest part of the balloon, making it less strong. If you put a pin into it, a **rip** races around the surface of the balloon where the molecules are most **stretched**. Placing the tape on it stops that rip from happening.

Increased pressure at the edge of the tear makes the rip spread.

Be bold! Stick it through!

Will it go POP?

Skewered balloon

The secret of this trick is to prepare the balloon before you show anyone. Once all of the skewers are in place, you won't fail to amaze. Practice removing the balloon from the tube at the end of the trick without showing that it was twisted.

This tube is 5 x 3 in (13 x 8 cm)

! **Ask an adult** to use something sharp to make the holes.

1 Poke pairs of holes through the opposite sides of the tube—look at the box (bottom) to see where you should place them.

Add some decoration.

2 Paint the tube silver, to make it look like metal, then decorate it.

Give it a twist and

Add some decoration to your tube.

slip on the tube.

3 Blow up a long balloon, but not too much, or you will not be able to twist it. Twist the balloon in the middle and cover the twist with the tube.

What? No pop?

4 Push the skewers through, avoiding the twisted center. You may have to push back the balloon with your thumb to help get the skewers through.

5 To perform the trick, set up the balloon with the skewers before you start your baffling performance. Pull the skewers out slowly, one at a time. Secretly untwist the balloon as you remove it from the tube.

What's the secret?

Twist the balloon in the middle to keep it from being skewered. But don't tell anyone! Most magic tricks deceive our eyes—it only looks as if the magic is happening.

Don't pull the sticks out too fast, or the balloon may pop.

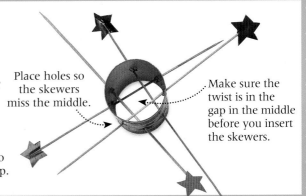

Place holes so the skewers miss the middle.

Make sure the twist is in the gap in the middle before you insert the skewers.

Balancir

Amaze an audience by balanci
pet butterflies on the tips of
straws, or even your nos
float, as if by

You will ne

- Tracing pa
- Cardboard •
Glue • Two sma
- Safety scis

They can float anywhere— make lots and lots!

Attach weight here.

Use glue to stick a small coin or washer to both wing tips.

Fly template

Use this outline to make your floating pet butterfly.

- Fold a piece of tracing paper in half and draw around the dotted line.
- Cut out this wing shape and open out the tracing paper.
- Trace the whole shape onto a piece of thin cardboard.

 Ask an adult to help with the scissors.

Fold the tracing paper here

Doing the trick

To ensure that the audience is totally confused, hand everyone a butterfly without the weights attached. People will be baffled when they can only balance it in the middle of its body!

Use thin cardboard, such as a cereal box.

Make sure

both sides are exactly the same.

Ask an adult

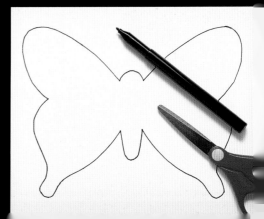

butterflies

Don't tell anyone the secret!

What's the science?

Without weights, the butterfly balances when both sides are being pulled down by the force of gravity in exactly equal amounts. If your finger is slightly to one side, the butterfly will fall off, since the forces on each side are not equal. It is hard to find the place where it balances—**the center of gravity**. When you add weights, the center of gravity is now halfway between the weights—on the nose of the butterfly. The paper wings droop down when the weights are added, which makes the butterfly bottom-heavy—it has a low center of gravity. This makes it harder to tip over and much easier to balance.

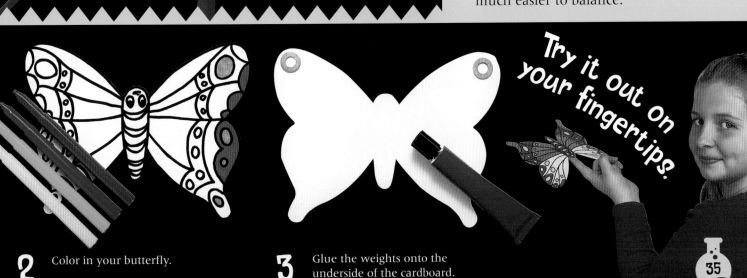

Try it out on your fingertips.

2 Color in your butterfly.

3 Glue the weights onto the underside of the cardboard.

Bubbling chemicals

Believe it or not, there are magic ingredients in your very own kitchen. You just need to know which ones to mix together to get explosive results!

⚠ Ask an adult

All of the ingredients are quite safe, but most of the mixtures, such as this one with vinegar, taste really yucky. So, don't drink them!

You will need:

- Baking soda
- Salt • Vinegar
- Food coloring
- Carbonated beverage
- A tray
- A small glass

What's the science?

When you open a bottle of soda you hear a **whooshing** sound. This is the sound of **carbon dioxide gas** escaping. The gas is what makes the drink fizzy. At the factory, **the gas is forced into the drink under high pressure**, which makes it dissolve in the liquid. When you release the lid, the **carbon dioxide slowly escapes from the liquid by forming bubbles.** Adding salt makes bubbles form faster, because the crystals have a rough surface that allows more bubbles to grow on them. The bubbles all rush to the top of the liquid together, making the frothy overflow.

Bubble and fizz

For an instant fizz, simply fill a small glass with any kind of carbonated drink. Place the glass on a tray to reduce the mess. Next, all you have to do is pour a teaspoon of salt on top. Add some food coloring to create multicolored bubbles.

Pour salt into the drink.

Watch it fizz all over.

Instant inflation

Amaze an audience by telling them that you will blow up a balloon without blowing at all.

First, pour some vinegar into a bottle.

Next, pour a teaspoon of baking soda powder into a balloon and stretch the balloon over the bottle's neck.

Don't let the soda out yet!

Pick up the balloon and empty out the baking soda.

As the baking soda mixes with the vinegar, it creates bubbles of carbon dioxide gas that escape into the balloon, making the balloon blow up. Let's hope there's no explosion!

You can also do this trick with yeast, sugar, and warm water.

Add the secret ingredient... and release the magic!

It has blown up by itself; no one touched it. It's still growing. Look!

Paper folding

How can you turn a flat, flimsy piece of paper into a sturdy box? How can you make paper fly? Experiment with paper folding—how many folds can you make?

You will need:

- Lots of paper
- Stapler
- Safety scissors

Use different paper sizes for big and small boxes. You can try out newspaper, comics, or construction paper.

What's the science?

Try folding a sheet of paper in half as many times as you can. How many times can you manage? No matter how hard you try, you can probably only fold the paper six or seven times. This is because **every time you fold the paper it becomes twice as thick**. Eventually, the paper has too small an area and is too thick to bend without a lot of effort. The record stands at 13 folds, using a very long piece of paper.

Paper is made from wood fibers and water that have been pulped together.

Perform PAPER tricks

Fold and hold—just a few folds and tucks, and a flat piece of paper becomes a strong box.

1 Fold a rectangle of paper in half and half again four times to make 16 squares. Then unfold it.

2 Bring the top and bottom flaps into the center.

3 Fold each corner down two-thirds to the center.

4 Fold the central edges of the paper level with the corners.

5 Turn the edges of the paper back to make flaps.

6 Hold the center of the two sides and pull them apart.

7 Pinch each corner from top to bottom to help form the shape of the box.

Open up!

8

9 Cut a wide strip of paper for a handle.

Staple the handle to each side.

Use patterned paper or paint a piece yourself.

Watch paper fly!

Make a paper airplane—a few simple folds and it flies!

1 Take a rectangle of paper and fold it in half.

2 Turn down one corner, as shown.

3 Fold the same corner down again.

4 Now, fold the top part down to make a wing.

5 Create the other wing.

6 Repeat the folds on the other half of the paper.

7 Open out the wings, turn the plane over, and whiz it across the room!

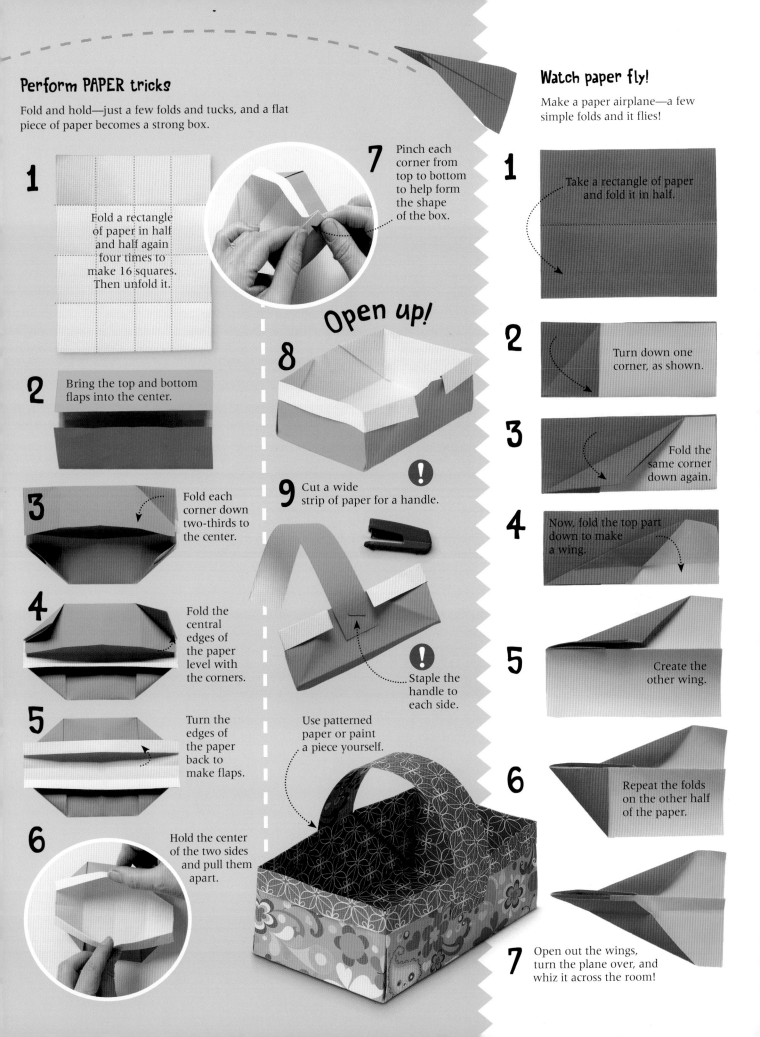

Mysterious metal

Some metals, like steel and iron, are attracted to a magnet by the force of magnetism. A strong magnet pulls on steel objects with a lot of force. It might even be able to make a small steel object move toward it without touching it!

❗ Ask an adult
to help with the scissors and stong glue.

You will need:

- Magnets • Cans • Toys
- Jar lids • Strong glue
- Cardboard • Paper clips
  - Paper fastener
  - Safety scissors
  - Felt

Test your metal

Find out whether metals are magnetic by touching a magnet onto various objects—if it sticks, they're magnetic.

Gone fishing!

Cut fish shapes out of thin cardboard and fasten a steel paper clip or paper fastener onto them. Tie a magnet to a piece of string. Tie the string to a pencil, then race your friends to pick up the fish.

Can containers

Tin-plated steel cans can be reused for storage. Because they are metal, they can be decorated with magnets. You can even spell out what is in the cans using letter magnets.

❗ Ask an adult
to cut the top off the can. Make sure it's clean and free from sharp edges. Ask an adult to glue some felt over the edge.

Homemade fridge magnets

Glue a magnet to the top of a jar or bottle lid, then glue a small toy to the other side. Stick your magnets onto cans or even the fridge door.

❗ Choking hazard
Do not leave small magnets lying around or unattended. Never put a magnet in your mouth.

Reuse lids from jars

Magnets

Strong glue

Small toys

Make a moving picture

1 Make a base by cutting out a piece of thin cardboard—for instance, use the back of a cereal box.

Decorate the background.

❷ Cut out cat shapes from thin cardboard.

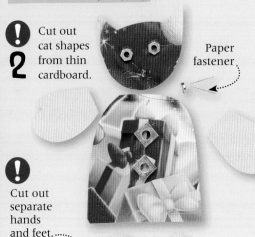

Paper fastener

❶ Cut out separate hands and feet.

Paper fastener

3 Push a paper fastener through the face to make the cat's nose. Then push it through the body.

Back of picture

Attach the cat to the cardboard by pressing the paper fastener through the cardboard.

4 Next, make four chains of four paper clips each. Attach these to the cat's hands and feet, then its body.

Crazy cat—make him dance!

5 To make the picture work, hold a magnet to the back of the cardboard and move it around. This will attract the metal on your picture and the character will jump around.

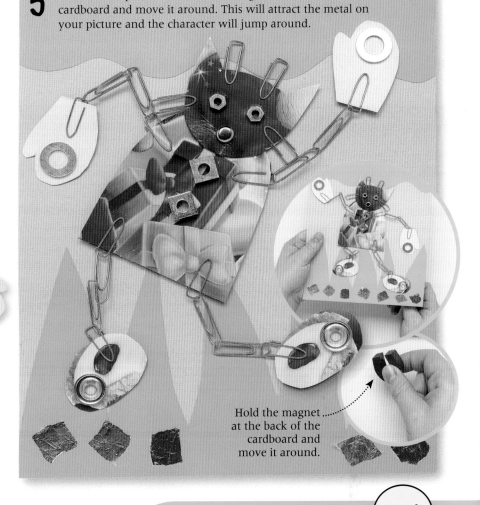

Hold the magnet at the back of the cardboard and move it around.

What's the science?

Magnets are special metals that can create an **invisible force field** around themselves. This force is strong enough to attract other magnetic objects to them. The way the force flows around the magnet creates a **"pole"** at each end. Each pole attracts its opposite pole. Magnetic metals have poles as well, so the poles on the metal will be attracted to the opposite poles on the magnet and they will stick firmly together.

... North pole

... Force field

N

S

South pole ...

Unmixable liquids

Do you want to decorate your own wrapping paper or origami paper? All you need is science! Oil paints dissolve in oil but not in water. Oil floats on water. This means you can float oily paint on top of water and transfer the paint onto paper to make some beautiful, marbled patterns.

Many colored pigments used in paint are made from natural substances, such as rocks, clay, berries, and leaves.

Before you start

In a well ventilated room, make some pots of paint mixture in different colors. Squeeze a blob of oil paint into a pot and add four capfuls of turpentine. Mix them together. The paint will become very thin.

! Ask an adult

to mix the paint with turpentine. Wash your hands properly after touching the turpentine and paint mixture.

Disposable baking pan with water

Spoon

Paint pots

Turpentine

Oil paints

Paper towel

White paper

Toothpick

Newspaper

 42

3 Float the paper on the surface and gently push down to help it make contact.

4 Pick up the corners and quickly lift out the paper.

1 Pour about 1 in (3 cm) of water into the pan. Add small spoonfuls of each paint color.

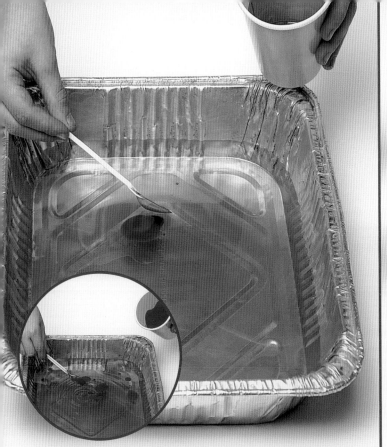

2 With a toothpick, swirl the paint gently in the water, but don't mix it too much.

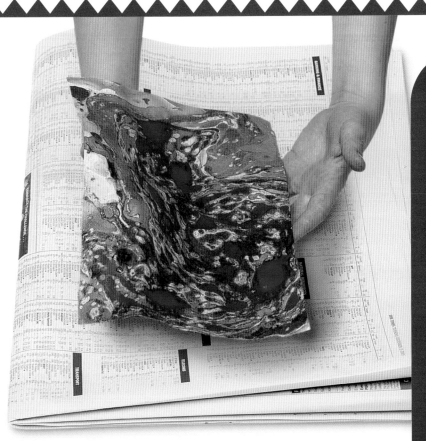

5 Leave the paper to dry flat on a thick layer of newspaper. Wash your hands properly after touching the turpentine and paint mixture.

What's the science?

Oil and water don't mix, which is why the oil paint floats on top of the water. This happens because **water molecules are tightly packed together**, making the water more dense (thick), so that it sinks to the bottom. The oil molecules are not as closely packed as those of the water, so they float on top. **Oil doesn't dissolve in water**, so even if you stir them together they will eventually separate into two layers.

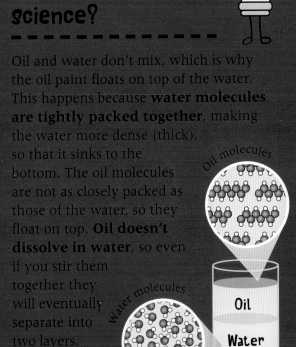

Oil molecules

Water molecules

Oil

Water

Bubbly bread

Adding yeast to flour and water wakes up the beast that is yeast! Yes, yeast is a microorganism. It might look like a powder, but it is actually full of tiny living things.

You will need:

Butter or margarine 2 tbsp

Granary bread flour 1¾ cups

White bread flour 1¾ cups

1 packet fast-acting yeast (2 tsp)

1 tsp brown sugar 1 tsp salt

Warm water 1¼ cups

A beaten egg for a glossy finish

3 tsp sesame seeds

3 tsp poppy seeds

3 tsp sunflower seeds

3 tsp pumpkin seeds

Makes 12 rolls

Bread tips

Yeast likes warmth to help it grow. Follow these tips to ensure that your bread rises.
• If all the things you work with are warm, such as the bowl and the room, this will help.
• Make sure the water isn't too hot. Hot water will kill the yeast and your bread won't rise.

Equipment:
• Mixing bowl
• Knife
• Wooden spoon
• Plastic wrap
• Baking sheet
• Pastry brush
• Cooling rack

What's the science?

One of the ingredients in dough is yeast. **Yeast is a living thing—it is a type of fungus** and is related to mushrooms and molds. Bakers add yeast to bread because it feeds on the sugars in flour and **produces bubbles of carbon dioxide gas.** This gas makes the dough expand to double its size. Baking traps the gas as the dough hardens in the heat, leaving you with a light, spongy texture to your bread.

1 Put the flours, yeast, sugar, and salt in a bowl and rub in the butter until the mixture looks like bread crumbs.

Use your hands to roll the dough into a ball.

Mix it up.

2 Make a well and pour in the water.

3 Mix with a wooden spoon until the dough comes away from the bowl.

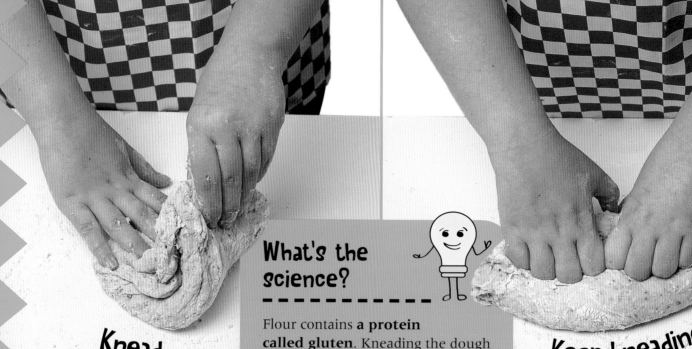

Knead the dough.

4 Sprinkle some flour on the work surface. Stretch the dough and fold it over.

What's the science?

Flour contains **a protein called gluten**. Kneading the dough makes the gluten soft and stretchy so that it can **trap the bubbles of carbon dioxide gas being produced by the yeast**. Without kneading, the dough goes flat because the gas bubbles escape.

Keep kneading.

5 Press your knuckles into the dough. Add more flour, if needed. Repeat steps 4 and 5 for 6 minutes.

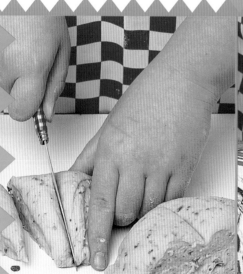

Divide it up.

! **Ask an adult** to help with the knife.

6 Make the dough into a ball and cut it into 12 even-sized pieces. Roll each into a small ball and place on a greased baking sheet.

! **7** Cover with plastic wrap and leave in a warm place for about 40 minutes to rise. Preheat the oven to 425°F (220°C).

8 When the rolls have doubled in size, they are ready to decorate. Brush them with beaten egg. Each roll then needs 1 tsp of a seed sprinkled over it.

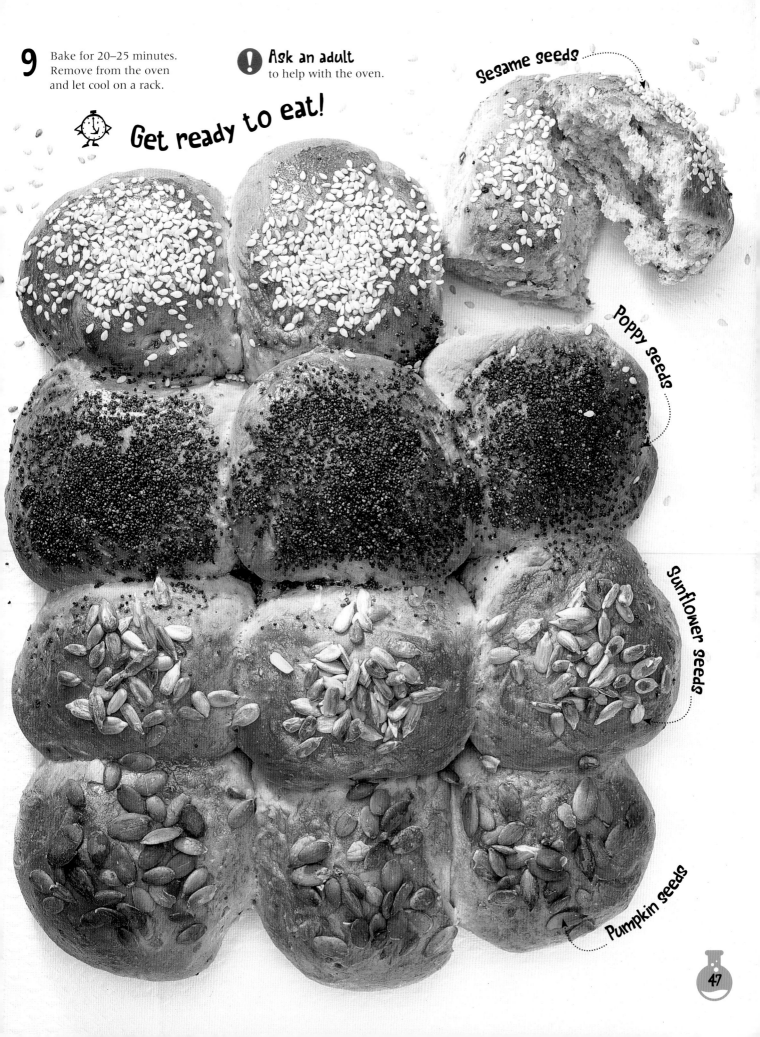

9 Bake for 20–25 minutes. Remove from the oven and let cool on a rack.

! **Ask an adult** to help with the oven.

Get ready to eat!

Sesame seeds

Poppy seeds

Sunflower seeds

Pumpkin seeds

Tasting zingy!

Squeezed to meet you!

This lemonade recipe will make just over one quart. It may be tangy, so add sugar or extra water until it tastes good. The best thing to do is experiment.

Drink up

Your lemonade will only keep for two days in the fridge. Make sure you drink it quickly!

You will need:

- 3 organic lemons
- 1 quart water
- Sugar, to taste

- Cutting board
- Sharp knife
- Measuring cup
- Blender
- Large bowl
- Strainer
- Large spoon
- Funnel
- Bottle

Making lemonade

Scrub all the lemons well, since you will be using the whole fruit— even the rind!

❗ Ask an adult
to help with the knife.

❗ Ask an adult
to help with the blender.

1 Wash the lemons and remove the ends and seeds. Carefully chop each into eight pieces.

2 Put the lemons into a blender and add some of the water.

3 Blend until the mixture is smooth.

Tasting with our tongues

Taste is one of our wonderful senses. Our tongues are covered in tiny bumps, called taste buds. They sense lots of different substances so we can taste the difference between foods. Some people have more taste buds than others, so they can taste more flavors.

What's the science?

Put your **tongue** against the cut side of a lemon. That tangy, sharp taste is a shock, isn't it? Lemons are **sour** because they contain **citric acid**, which activates the **taste buds** on your tongue that detect sour flavors.

All citrus fruits contain citric acid, but some seem less sour because they contain more sugar. Try tasting grapefruit, limes, oranges, tangerines, and lemons together—which is the sweetest?

4 Pour the mixture into a strainer.

5 Let the juice drain through, pressing it with the back of a spoon.

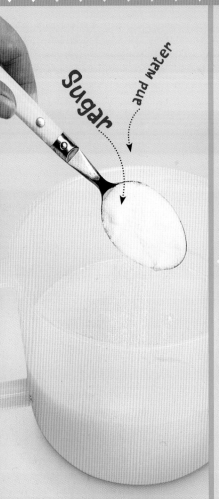

Sugar *and water*

6 Add some sugar, to taste, and the remaining water.

It's best to keep your lemonade in a bottle in the fridge.

Gently pour through a funnel.

Hold the bottle tightly.

7 Bottle your lemonade.

Exploding corn!

When you pop a kernel of corn, you change it permanently. Water escapes, as it is heated into a gas, and the shape of the kernel is altered forever... before it is eaten!

Pop
Pop
Pop

Pop
Pop

Corn is not the only exploding grain. Barley, rice, and quinoa can also be popped.

50

Pop*

*Pop   *Pop

Cook for about a minute, or until there are no more pops.

What's the science?

What makes a kernel of corn explode when you heat it? Well, inside every kernel is a mixture of **oil, water, protein,** and **starch.** When you heat the kernels, the **water tries to turn into steam** but is held in by the tough outer husk. The rest of the seed turns into a paste. When the seed husk can't contain the steam any more, it splits apart. The steam is released so fast **it blows the paste into a foam, which cools and solidifies**.

 Ask an adult to pour the popcorn into the very hot pan.

1 Heat the oil. Let it get really hot before you add the corn kernels.

2 Put on the lid and listen for pops. When you hear some popping, gently shake the pan.

You won't need any heat under the pan.

3 Turn off the heat and take a peek. Take the pan off the burner to cool.

4 Stir in the butter, and the popcorn is ready. If you like, sprinkle sugar or salt on top while the popcorn is in the pan.

Bags of flavor
For some exciting tastes to add to your buttered popcorn:
1. Pour your popcorn into a clean plastic bag.
2. Add grated cheese or a mix of dried herbs.
3. Squeeze the top of the bag, shake it well, then serve.

You will need:

Self-rising flour
1 cup

Butter (room temperature)
8 tbsp

Sugar
⅔ cup

2 eggs

1 tsp
baking powder

1 tsp
vanilla
extract

Makes 24
cupcakes

Equipment:

- Mixing bowl
- Electric mixer
- 2 muffin pans
- Cupcake liners
- Cooling rack
- Strainer

Cupcake science

What's the science?

The secret to making a good cake is to make lots of **bubbles** and hold them in the mixture. **Beating** the ingredients adds air bubbles to the mix. **Baking powder** produces more bubbles when it mixes with the wet egg. All the bubbles become trapped in the sticky, stretchy batter formed by the flour and eggs. As the cupcakes bake, the mixture hardens around the bubbles and turns into a spongy solid.

There is a lot of science in a cake. Baking is all about chemistry and how the ingredients combine. You have to get everything just right to create a cake that is light, fluffy, and scrumptious.

Preheat the oven to 375°F (190°C). Ask an adult to help you with this.

1 Sift the flour and baking powder together. Sifting adds air and gets rid of lumps.

Add everything else.

2 Beat the eggs and add them, along with the butter, sugar, and vanilla extract, to the flour.

Beat until the mix is creamy. Does it drop off a spoon?

Ask an adult to help with the electric mixer.

3 If it drops off easily in a dollop, then the batter is ready.

Fill up the liners.

4 Put a teaspoon of batter in each liner. Ask an adult to bake the cupcakes for 20 minutes.

⚠5 Ask an adult to take the muffin pan out of the oven once the cupcakes are golden brown.

6 Leave to cool. Now decorate!

Rainbow icing

Mix up lots of little bowls of different colored icing. For green icing, mix yellow and blue; for orange, combine yellow and red. Use anything sweet to decorate the cupcake tops, such as candied cherries, raisins, and candies.

You will need:

- 1 tbsp powdered sugar
- 1 tsp water
- 1 drop food coloring
- Candies
- Writing icing

To ice
4 cupcakes

1 Stir together the water, food coloring, and sugar.

2 Drop a small dollop of icing onto the center of the cupcake and let it spread.

Cherry

3 Decorate it with anything sweet. Use tubes of icing for extra patterns.

What's the science?

Baking the cupcakes sets all the ingredients. First, it makes the **bubbles expand** and double in size. As the heat increases, the **egg and flour proteins begin to harden**. The top and edges of the cupcake turn brown as the sugar caramelizes. The **temperature is crucial**: if the oven is too cool, the the gas bubbles escape before the batter sets, leaving a flat, heavy cupcake. If it is too hot, then the outside bakes before the middle, producing a cracked, peaked cupcake.

It's ready when you can turn the bowl upside-down over your he without the whites sliding out.

3 Keep beating until the whites are stiff and form trails around the beaters.

! **Ask an adult** to help with the electric mixer.

Use a large, clean bowl.

1 Separate the white of the egg from the yolk. Pour into a bowl.

Beat egg whites at top speed.

2 The whites turn frothy as you beat them.

Mix up meringues

How can liquid egg whites become solid? Add sugar, beat in some air, add a little heat to evaporate the water, and you have crunchy meringues.

Grease the sheet, then cover it with parchment paper.

! **Preheat** the oven to 275°F (140°C). Ask an adult to help with this step.

7 Spoon out the mixture and swirl it to form rough peaks.

Bake in the oven for 2 hours.

! 8 Let the meringues dry out for a few hours.

..Use a lower
speed to beat
in the sugar.

..Mixture should
stand up in
firm points.

4 Next, add the sugar, one tablespoon at a time, while beating. Repeat until all the sugar is used up.

5 When all the sugar is combined, give the mixture a final whisk.

6 Now, the mixture is ready. It should look smooth and glossy.

You will need:

Sugar
⅔ cup

2 large egg whites

Electric mixer

Mixing bowl

Teaspoon

Soup spoon

Parchment paper

Baking sheet

Pastry brush

Pile them high!

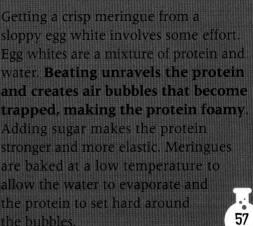

What's the science?

Getting a crisp meringue from a sloppy egg white involves some effort. Egg whites are a mixture of protein and water. **Beating unravels the protein and creates air bubbles that become trapped, making the protein foamy.** Adding sugar makes the protein stronger and more elastic. Meringues are baked at a low temperature to allow the water to evaporate and the protein to set hard around the bubbles.

Melt in your mouth!

Chocolate makes the best cookies, and it's scientific, too. It melts in the oven and solidifies when the cookies cool. It then melts on your tongue because of the heat of your mouth. Mmmmm... science tastes good!

Makes 12 cookies

You will need:

Brown sugar ½ cup

Sugar ⅓ cup

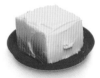
Butter 8 tbsp

1 Egg

All-purpose flour 1⅓ cups

Baking soda 1 tsp

Chocolate chunks 7 oz (175 g)

Chocolate is made from the fruit of the cacao tree. Raw beans are bitter, so they are roasted, ground up, and mixed with sugar and milk to make something truly delicious.

Equipment

Mixing bowl

Spoon

Knife

Wooden spoon

Pastry brush

Baking tray

Cooling rack

Soft butter is easier to mix with the sugar.

1 Cream the butter and sugar together until fluffy.

Add beaten egg.

2 Mix in the egg. Ask an adult to preheat the oven to 375°F (190°C).

3 Stir in the flour and mix all the ingredients thoroughly.

4 Add the chocolate. Get help chopping it into chunks.

Place some extra chunks on top of the dough before baking.

5 Place four heaping spoonfuls of dough onto the baking sheet.

6 Bake for 10–12 minutes. Ask an adult to take the cookies out of the oven.

7 Let the cookies cool before moving them to a rack. Clean the baking sheet for the next batch.

Yum, yum

What's the science?

One of the wonderful things about chocolate is the way it melts in your mouth. That is because it **melts at** a temperature that is very close to **body temperature**. It does this because it contains **cocoa butter**, which is a type of fat found in cocoa beans. Dark, milk, and white chocolate all contain different amounts of cocoa butter.

Glossary

Acid

Acids are sharp-tasting or sour substances. Lemon juice, soft drinks, and vinegar are all mild acids.

Atom

Atoms are the invisible building blocks of the universe. They can join together to form molecules that make up most of the things you see around you, and even some of the ones you can't see, such as gases.

Baking powder

This is a mixture of chemicals used in baking to make a cake rise. It works by producing carbon dioxide gas bubbles to make a cake light and spongy.

Baking soda

Bicarbonate is one of the ingredients of baking soda. It reacts with an acid to produce carbon dioxide gas.

Buoyancy

The ability of something to float is called its buoyancy. It depends on the weight of the object and how much liquid is underneath pushing it upward.

Carbon dioxide

Carbon dioxide is a colorless, odorless gas. Naturally found in the atmosphere, it is also produced by plants and animals, and by chemical reactions.

Citric acid

This is the acid found in citrus fruits, such as lemons and oranges.

Crystal

A crystal is a solid material whose atoms are arranged in a regular pattern. Salt, sugar, and ice are all examples of crystals.

Energy

Energy is the ability of something to do work. This work can take different forms: heat, light, movement, gravity, chemical, and nuclear are just some types of energy. Energy can be converted from one form to another and stored until it is needed.

Floating

Objects float when they have buoyancy. This can happen when the object is placed into a liquid or into the air (if it is light enough). Objects that are too heavy will sink.

Force

A force is usually a push or a pull between two objects. Forces always happen in pairs—when one object exerts a force on another object, it experiences a force in return. Forces can make things move, change their speed and direction, or change their shape.

Gluten

Gluten is a protein found in cereals and grains, such as wheat, barley, and rye. It is produced during bread making and makes the dough elastic and stretchy, giving the baked bread its spongy texture.

Gravity

Gravity is an invisible force pulling objects toward the center of the Earth. It also keeps the planets orbiting the sun.

Herb

A herb is a plant whose leaves, seeds, or flowers can be used for perfume or to flavor food or medicine.

Kneading

This is the process of pulling and stretching a dough to encourage gluten to form faster.

Light ray

A ray is the path that light travels on between two points.

Magnet

A magnet is a piece of iron or other material that can attract another magnetic object to it by the invisible force of magnetism.

Magnetic field

This is the region around a magnet where the magnetic force will work. The field creates a force that can pull two magnets together or push them apart.

Metal

Metal is a solid substance that is hard, usually shiny, and can allow heat or electricity to pass through it. Metals can be bent or pulled into shapes.

Molecule

A molecule is a group of two or more atoms that are joined together by internal bonds. The atoms can all be the same or different.

Moving energy

This is the energy that an object has after a force has been applied to it to make it move. It is also known as kinetic energy.

Nitrogen

Nitrogen is a colorless gas that makes up most of the atmosphere. Its atoms are vital to all living things, since they are a key ingredient of proteins.

Nutrients

A nutrient is a substance used by living things so that they can survive, grow, and reproduce.

Pole

A pole is the region of a magnet where the magnetic field is strongest. There are usually two poles, one at each end of the magnet. They are described as the north and south poles. A north pole will attract the south pole of another magnet and stick fast. Two north or south poles put close together repel each other and cannot be pushed together.

Pressure

This is a physical force that is exerted on or against an object by something that is in contact with it. For example, blowing air into a balloon creates pressure on the rubber of the balloon, causing it to stretch. If the pressure is too great, the balloon will burst.

Protein

Proteins are huge molecules that are vital to all living things. They are essential to the structure and function of cells, tissues, and organs in the body of animals and plants.

Solid

A solid is a hard substance that holds its shape until acted on by a strong force.

Sour

This describes one of the basic taste sensations. Sour things have a sharp, sometimes unpleasant, taste or smell that is the opposite of sweet. Lemons and vinegar are sour.

Starch

Starch is an odorless and tasteless white substance found in plants, especially grains and potatoes. It is used by plants as a source of energy.

Steam

This is water that has turned into a gas after being heated to its boiling point. It is also called water vapor.

Stored energy

Stored (or potential) energy is the energy that an object is said to have when it is not doing any work. If a force is applied to the object, the stored energy will be converted into another form of energy.

Taste bud

A taste bud is one of the tiny bumps on the tongue that allows you to taste sweet, sour, salty, bitter, and savory flavors.

Transparent

Something that is easy to see through—such as clear glass or plastic—is said to be transparent.

Index

THIS EDITION
Design and Text Jane Bull
Science Consultant and Text Jules Pottle
Senior Editor Carrie Love
US Senior Editor Shannon Beatty
US Editor Margaret Parrish
Senior Art Editors Charlotte Bull, Kanika Kalra
Assistant Editors Agey George, Syed Tuba Javed
Jacket Designers Alison Tutton, Rashika Kachroo
DTP Designers Sachin Gupta, Rajdeep Singh
Project Picture Researcher Rituraj Singh
Managing Editors Penny Smith, Monica Saigal
Managing Art Editor Ivy Sengupta
Production Editor Becky Fallowfield
Production Controller Leanne Burke
Delhi Creative Heads Glenda Fernandes, Malavika Talukder
Deputy Art Director Mabel Chan
Publishing Director Sarah Larter

FIRST EDITION
Design and Text Jane Bull
Photographer Andy Crawford
Editor Violet Peto
Science Editor Wendy Horobin
Designer Sadie Thomas
Design Assistant Eleanor Bates
Producer, Pre-Production Dragana Puvacic
Producer John Casey
Jacket Designer Alison Tutton
Jacket Coordinator Francesca Young
Managing Editor Penny Smith
Managing Art Editor Mabel Chan
Publisher Mary Ling
Art Director Jane Bull

This American Edition, 2023
Published in Great Britain by Dorling Kindersley Limited
DK, One Embassy Gardens, 8 Viaduct Gardens, London SW11 7BW

US edition first published in the United States in 2018
Previously published as *Crafty Science*

Distributed by DK Publishing, an imprint of Penguin Random House LLC
1745 Broadway, 20th Floor, New York, NY 10019

Copyright © 2018, 2023 Dorling Kindersley Limited
DK, a Division of Penguin Random House LLC
23 24 25 26 27 10 9 8 7 6 5 4 3 2
002–334139–Jul/2023

A catalog record for this book
is available from the Library of Congress.
ISBN 978-0-7440-8042-1

Material used in this book was first published in:
The Christmas Book (2002), *The Magic Book* (2002),
The Rainy Day Book (2003), *The Gardening Book* (2003),
The Cooking Book (2003), *The Sunny Day Book* (2004),
The Crafty Art Book (2004) *The Baking Book* (2005),
and *Make It!* (2008).

DK books are available at special discounts when purchased
in bulk for sales promotions, premiums, fund-raising, or educational
use. For details, contact: DK Publishing Special Markets,
1745 Broadway, 20th Floor, New York, NY 10019
SpecialSales@dk.com

Printed and bound in China

For the curious
www.dk.com

MIX
Paper | Supporting
responsible forestry
FSC™ C018179

This book was made with Forest
Stewardship Council™ certified
paper—one small step in DK's
commitment to a sustainable future.
**For more information go to
www.dk.com/our-green-pledge**

64

DISCLAIMER: The recipes may contain ingredients to
which you or a friend are allergic or otherwise not part of your
recommended diet. Each reader of the book needs to be aware
of their own dietary requirements and the publisher cannot take
any responsibility for any adverse reactions you may have to the
recipes in this book. Please be aware that substituting ingredients
will not always give you the same result for the recipe.

Acknowledgments

Dorling Kindersley would like to thank the following
people for their assistance in the preparation of this book:
Niharika Prabhakar and Radhika Haswani for editorial
support, Bhagyashree Nayak and Mansi Dwivedi for
design support, Caryn Jenner for proofreading the text,
Helen Peters for compiling the index, and Anne Damerell
for legal assistance.

Picture Credits

The publisher would like to thank the following for
their kind permission to reproduce their photographs:

(Key: a-above; b-below/bottom; c-centre; f-far; l-left;
r-right; t-top)

4 Dreamstime.com: Goldenleaf (tr); Melica (cla).
5 Dreamstime.com: Jiradelta (cla); Chadchai Krisadapong
(cra). **Eddy Hyde:** (ca). **7 Getty Images:** Martin Barraud
/ OJO Images (tr); Stuart McClymont / The Image Bank
(tl); Robert Stahl / The Image Bank (bl). **12 iStockphoto.
com:** akinshin (t/bubbles). **13 iStockphoto.com:**
wundervisuals (main image). **31 Dreamstime.com:**
Alexstar (tc, cr). **36 Dreamstime.com:** Shutterfree,
Llc / R. Gino Santa Maria (tl)

Cover images: Front and Back: **Dreamstime.com:**
Vector Moon
All other images © Dorling Kindersley

See you
again soon!